POEMS
FOR CHRISTMAS

POEMS
FOR CHRISTMAS

Selected by Neil Philip
Illustrated by John Lawrence

St. Martin's Press
New York

For Leslie Stoker
N.P.

For John and Rob
J.L.

CONTENTS

MUMMER'S SONG

Now welcome, welcome Christmas
With a right good cheer
Away dumps, away dumps
Nor come you not here
And I wish you a merry Christmas
And a Happy New Year.

TRADITIONAL

A CHILD'S CALENDAR

No visitors in January.
A snowman smokes a cold pipe in the yard.

They stand about like ancient women,
The February hills.
They have seen many a coming and going, the hills.

In March, Moorfea is littered
With knock-kneed lambs.

Daffodils at the door in April,
Three shawled Marys.
A lark splurges in galilees of sky.

And in May
A russet stallion shoulders the hill apart.
The mares tremble.

The June bee
Bumps in the pane with a heavy bag of plunder.

Strangers swarm in July
With cameras, binoculars, bird books.

He thumped the crag in August,
A blind blue whale.

September crofts get wrecked in blond surges.
They struggle, the harvesters.
They drag loaf and ale-kirn into winter.

In October the fishmonger
Argues, pleads, threatens at the shore.

Nothing in November
But tinkers at the door, keening, with cans.

Some December midnight
Christ, lord, lie warm in our byre.
Here are stars, an ox, poverty enough.

GEORGE MACKAY BROWN

SUMMER IS GONE

My tidings for you: the stag bells,
Winter snows, summer is gone.

Wind high and cold, low the sun,
Short his course, sea running high.

Deep-red the bracken, its shape all gone —
The wild-goose has raised his wonted cry.

Cold has caught the wings of birds;
Season of ice: these are my tidings.

ANONYMOUS
Old Irish translated by Kuno Meyer

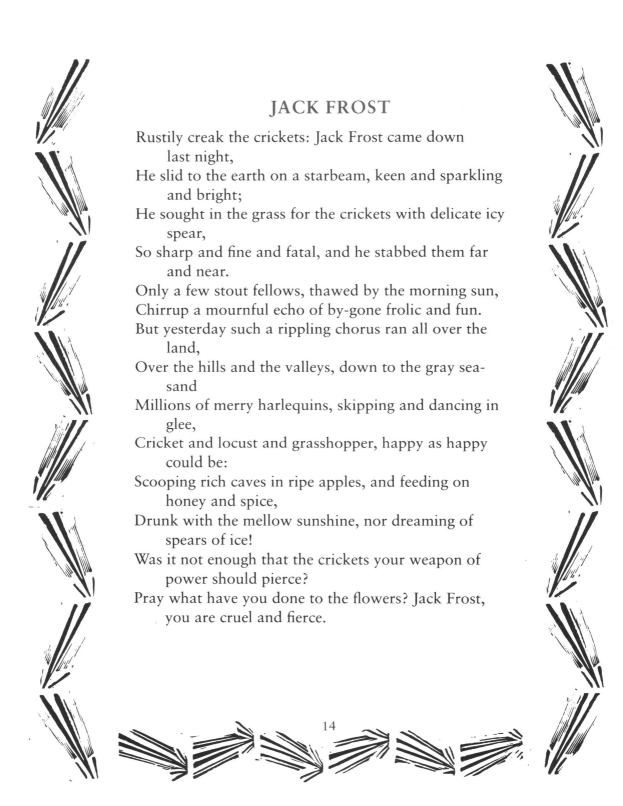

JACK FROST

Rustily creak the crickets: Jack Frost came down
    last night,
He slid to the earth on a starbeam, keen and sparkling
    and bright;
He sought in the grass for the crickets with delicate icy
    spear,
So sharp and fine and fatal, and he stabbed them far
    and near.
Only a few stout fellows, thawed by the morning sun,
Chirrup a mournful echo of by-gone frolic and fun.
But yesterday such a rippling chorus ran all over the
    land,
Over the hills and the valleys, down to the gray sea-
    sand
Millions of merry harlequins, skipping and dancing in
    glee,
Cricket and locust and grasshopper, happy as happy
    could be:
Scooping rich caves in ripe apples, and feeding on
    honey and spice,
Drunk with the mellow sunshine, nor dreaming of
    spears of ice!
Was it not enough that the crickets your weapon of
    power should pierce?
Pray what have you done to the flowers? Jack Frost,
    you are cruel and fierce.

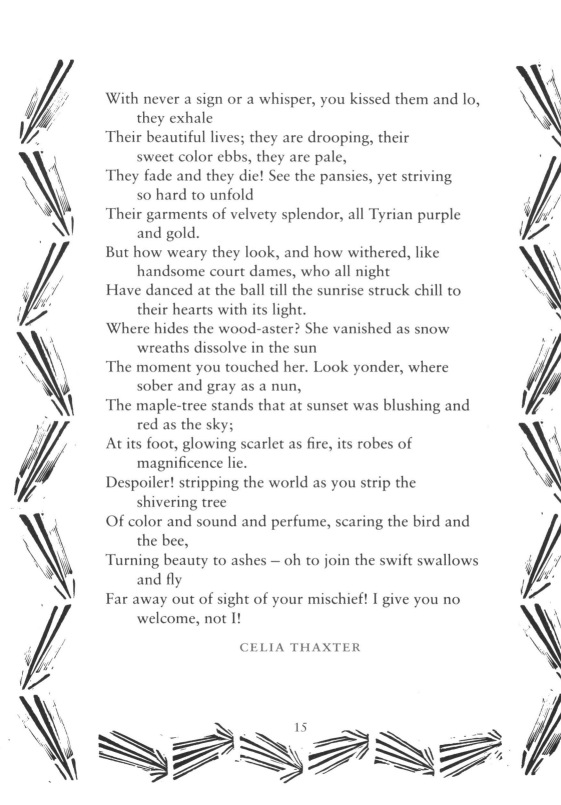

With never a sign or a whisper, you kissed them and lo,
   they exhale
Their beautiful lives; they are drooping, their
   sweet color ebbs, they are pale,
They fade and they die! See the pansies, yet striving
   so hard to unfold
Their garments of velvety splendor, all Tyrian purple
   and gold.
But how weary they look, and how withered, like
   handsome court dames, who all night
Have danced at the ball till the sunrise struck chill to
   their hearts with its light.
Where hides the wood-aster? She vanished as snow
   wreaths dissolve in the sun
The moment you touched her. Look yonder, where
   sober and gray as a nun,
The maple-tree stands that at sunset was blushing and
   red as the sky;
At its foot, glowing scarlet as fire, its robes of
   magnificence lie.
Despoiler! stripping the world as you strip the
   shivering tree
Of color and sound and perfume, scaring the bird and
   the bee,
Turning beauty to ashes – oh to join the swift swallows
   and fly
Far away out of sight of your mischief! I give you no
   welcome, not I!

CELIA THAXTER

CHRISTMAS WITH KING ARTHUR

FROM *Sir Gawain and the Green Knight*

This king lay at Camelot one Christmastide
With loyal lords, liegemen peerless,
Members rightly reckoned of the Round Table,
In splendid celebration, seemly and carefree.
There tussling in tournament time and again
Jousted in jollity these gentle knights,
Then in court carnival sang catches and danced;
For there the feasting flowed for fully fifteen days
With all the meat and merry-making men could devise,
Gladly ringing glee, glorious to hear
Debonair rejoicing by day, dancing at night!
All was happiness in the height in halls and chambers
For lords and their ladies, delectable joy.
With all delights on earth they housed there together,
The most renowned knights acknowledging Christ,
The loveliest ladies to live in all time,
And the comeliest king ever to keep court.
For this goodly gathering was in its golden age
        Far famed,
    Well graced by God's good will,
    With its mettlesome king acclaimed:
    So hardly a host on hill
    Could not with ease be named.

ANONYMOUS
translated by Brian Stone

STOPPING BY WOODS ON A SNOWY EVENING

Whose woods these are I think I know.
His house is in the village though;
He will not see me stopping here
To watch his woods fill up with snow.

My little horse must think it queer
To stop without a farmhouse near
Between the woods and frozen lake
The darkest evening of the year.

He gives his harness bells a shake
To ask if there is some mistake.
The only other sound's the sweep
Of easy wind and downy flake.

The woods are lovely, dark and deep.
But I have promises to keep,
And miles to go before I sleep,
And miles to go before I sleep.

ROBERT FROST

ON A NIGHT OF SNOW

Cat, if you go outdoors you must walk in the snow.
You will come back with little white shoes on your feet,
Little white slippers of snow that have heels of sleet.
Stay by the fire, my Cat. Lie still, do not go.
See how the flames are leaping and hissing low,
I will bring you a saucer of milk like a marguerite,
So white and so smooth, so spherical and so sweet –
Stay with me, Cat. Outdoors the wild winds blow.

Outdoors the wild winds blow, Mistress, and dark is the night.
Strange voices cry in the trees, intoning strange lore;
And more than cats move, lit by our eyes' green light,
On silent feet where the meadow grasses hang hoar –
Mistress, there are portents abroad of magic and might,
And things that are yet to be done. Open the door!

ELIZABETH COATSWORTH

WHY DOES IT SNOW?

"Why does it snow? Why does it snow?"
The children come crowding around me to know.
I said to my nephew, I said to my niece,
"It's just the old woman a-plucking her geese."

    With her riddle cum dinky dido,
    With her riddle cum dinky dee.

The old woman sits on a pillowy cloud,
She calls to her geese, and they come in a crowd;
A cackle, a wackle, a hiss and a cluck,
And then the old woman begins for to pluck.

    With her riddle cum dinky dido,
    With her riddle cum dinky dee.

The feathers go fluttering up in the air,
Until the poor geese are entirely bare;
A toddle, a waddle, a hiss and a cluck,
"You may grow some more if you have the good luck!"

    With your riddle cum dinky dido,
    With your riddle cum dinky dee.

The feathers go swirling around and around,
Then whirlicking, twirlicking, sink to the ground;
The farther they travel, the colder they grow,
And when they get down here, they've turned into snow.

    With their riddle cum dinky dido,
    With their riddle cum dinky dee.

LAURA E. RICHARDS

THE SNOW-MAN

Look! how the clouds are flying south!
   The wind pipes loud and shrill!
And high above the white drifts stands
   The snow-man on the hill.

Blow, wild wind from the icy north!
   Here's one who will not fear
To feel thy coldest touch, or shrink
   Thy loudest blast to hear!

Proud triumph of the school-boy's skill!
   Far rather would I be
A winter giant, ruling o'er
   A frosty realm, like thee,

And stand amidst the drifted snow,
   Like thee, a thing apart,
Than be a man who walks with men,
   But has a frozen heart!

MARIAN DOUGLAS

WHITE FIELDS

I

In the winter time we go
Walking in the fields of snow;

Where there is no grass at all;
Where the top of every wall,

Every fence, and every tree,
Is as white as white can be.

II

Pointing out the way we came,
— Every one of them the same —

All across the fields there be
Prints in silver filigree;

And our mothers always know,
By the footprints in the snow,

Where it is the children go.

JAMES STEPHENS

SONG

FROM *Love's Labours Lost*

When icicles hang by the wall,
   And Dick the shepherd blows his nail,
And Tom bears logs into the hall,
   And milk comes frozen home in pail;
When blood is nipp'd and ways be foul,
Then nightly sings the staring owl,
       To-whit! to-who!
     A merry note,
While greasy Joan doth keel the pot.

When all aloud the wind doth blow,
   And coughing drowns the parson's saw;
And birds sit brooding in the snow,
   And Marian's nose looks red and raw;
When roasted crabs hiss in the bowl,
Then nightly sings the staring owl,
       To-whit! to-who!
     A merry note,
While greasy Joan doth keel the pot.

WILLIAM SHAKESPEARE

SNOW-FLAKES

Out of the bosom of the Air,
    Out of the cloud-folds of her garments shaken,
Over the woodlands brown and bare,
    Over the harvest-fields forsaken,
        Silent, and soft, and slow
        Descends the snow.

Even as our cloudy fancies take
    Suddenly shape in some divine expression,
Even as the troubled heart doth make
    In the white countenance confession,
        The troubled sky reveals
        The grief it feels.

This is the poem of the air,
    Slowly in silent syllables recorded;
This is the secret of despair,
    Long in its cloudy bosom hoarded,
        Now whispered and revealed
        To wood and field.

HENRY WADSWORTH LONGFELLOW

CHRISTMAS SONG

Above the weary waiting world,
Asleep in chill despair,
There breaks a sound of joyous bells
Upon the frosted air.
And o'er the humblest rooftree, lo,
A star is dancing on the snow.

What makes the yellow star to dance
Upon the brink of night?
What makes the breaking dawn to glow
So magically bright, —
And all the earth to be renewed
With infinite beatitude?

The singing bells, the throbbing star,
The sunbeams on the snow,
And the awakening heart that leaps
New ecstasy to know, —
They all are dancing in the morn
Because a little child is born.

BLISS CARMAN

CHRISTMAS CARD

You have anti-freeze in the car, yes,
    But the shivering stars wade deeper.
Your scarf's tucked in under your buttons,
    But a dry snow ticks through the stubble.
Your knee-boots gleam in the fashion,
    But the moon must stay

        And stamp and cry
        As the holly the holly
        Hots its reds.

Electric blanket to comfort your bedtime
    The river no longer feels its stones.
Your windows are steamed by dumpling laughter
    The snowplough's buried on the drifted moor.
Carols shake your television
    And nothing moves on the road but the wind

        Hither and thither
        The wind and three
        Starving sheep.

Redwings from Norway rattle at the clouds
    But comfortless sneezers puddle in pubs.
The robin looks in at the kitchen window
    But all care huddles to hearths and kettles.
The sun lobs one wet snowball feebly
    Grim and blue

        The dusk of the coombe
        And the swamp woodland
        Sinks with the wren.

See old lips go purple and old brows go paler.
  The stiff crow drops in the midnight silence.
Sneezes grow coughs and coughs grow painful.
  The vixen yells in the midnight garden.
You wake with the shakes and watch your breathing
  Smoke in the moonlight – silent, silent.

      Your anklebone
      And your anklebone
      Lie big in the bed.

            TED HUGHES

LITTLE TREE

little tree
little silent Christmas tree
you are so little
you are more like a flower

who found you in the green forest
and were you very sorry to come away?
see   i will comfort you
because you smell so sweetly

i will kiss your cool bark
and hug you safe and tight
just as your mother would,
only don't be afraid

look   the spangles
that sleep all the year in a dark box
dreaming of being taken out and allowed to shine,
the balls the chains red and gold the fluffy threads,

put up your little arms
and i'll give them all to you to hold
every finger shall have its ring
and there won't be a single place dark or unhappy

then when you're quite dressed
you'll stand in the window for everyone to see
and how they'll stare!
oh but you'll be very proud

and my little sister and i will take hands
and looking up at our beautiful tree
we'll dance and sing
"Noel Noel"

E. E. CUMMINGS

30

MY FATHER PLAYED THE MELODEON

FROM *A Christmas Childhood*

My father played the melodeon
Outside at our gate;
There were stars in the morning east
And they danced to his music.

Across the wild bogs his melodeon called
To Lennons and Callans.
As I pulled on my trousers in a hurry
I knew some strange thing had happened.

Outside in the cow-house my mother
Made the music of milking;
The light of her stable-lamp was a star
And the frost of Bethlehem made it twinkle.

A water-hen screeched in the bog,
Mass-going feet
Crunched the wafer-ice on the pot-holes,
Somebody wistfully twisted the bellows wheel.

My child poet picked out the letters
On the grey stone,
In silver the wonder of a Christmas townland,
The winking glitter of a frosty dawn.

Cassiopeia was over
Cassidy's hanging hill,
I looked and three whin bushes rode across
The horizon – the Three Wise Kings.

An old man passing said:
"Can't he make it talk" –
The melodeon. I hid in the doorway
And tightened the belt of my box-pleated coat.

I nicked six nicks on the door-post
With my penknife's big blade –
There was a little one for cutting tobacco.
And I was six Christmasses of age.

My father played the melodeon,
My mother milked the cows,
And I had a prayer like a white rose pinned
On the Virgin Mary's blouse.

PATRICK KAVANAGH

THE CHERRY-TREE CAROL

Joseph was an old man,
  And an old man was he,
When he wedded Mary
  In the land of Galilee.

Joseph and Mary walked
  Through an orchard good,
Where was cherries and berries
  So red as any blood.

Joseph and Mary walked
  Through an orchard green,
Where was berries and cherries
  As thick as might be seen.

O then bespoke Mary
  So meek and so mild:
Pluck me one cherry, Joseph,
  For I am with child.

O then bespoke Joseph
  With words most unkind:
Let him pluck thee a cherry
  That brought thee with child.

O then bespoke the Babe
  Within his Mother's womb:
Bow down then the tallest tree
  For my Mother to have some.

Then bowed down the highest tree
  Unto his Mother's hand;
Then she cried, See, Joseph,
  I have cherries at command.

O then bespoke Joseph:
  I have done Mary wrong;
But cheer up, my dearest,
  And be not cast down.

Then Mary plucked a cherry
  As red as the blood,
Then Mary went home
  With her heavy load.

Then Mary took her Babe
  And sat him on her knee,
Saying, My dear Son, tell me
  What this world will be.

O I shall be as dead, Mother,
  As the stones in the wall;
O the stones in the streets, Mother,
  Shall mourn for me all.

Upon Easter-day, Mother,
  My uprising shall be;
O the sun and the moon, Mother,
  Shall both rise with me.

TRADITIONAL

MRS. KRISS KRINGLE

Oh, I laugh to hear what grown folk
   Tell the young folk of Kriss Kringle,
In the Northland, where unknown folk
   Love to feel the frost-wind tingle.

Yes, I laugh to hear the grown folk
   Tell you young folk how Kriss Kringle
Travels 'round the world like lone folk,
   None to talk with – always single!

Would a grim and grave old fellow
   (Not a chick nor child to care for)
Keep a heart so warm and mellow
   That all children he'd prepare for?

Do you think, my little maiden,
   He could ever guess your wishes –
That you'd find your stocking laden
   With a doll and set of dishes?

No; the truth is, some one whispers
   In the ear he hears the best with,
What to suit the youngest lispers,
   Boys and girls, and all the rest with.

Some one (ah, you guess in vain, dear!)
    Nestled close by old Kriss Kringle,
Laughs to see the prancing reindeer,
    Laughs to hear the sledge bells jingle.

Dear old lady, small and rosy!
    In the nipping, Christmas weather,
Nestled close, so warm and cozy,
    These two chat, for hours together.

So, if I were in your places,
    Rob and Hal, and Kate, and Mary,
I would be in the good graces
    Of this lovely, shy old fairy.

Still I laugh to hear the grown folk
    Tell you young folk how Kriss Kringle
Travels 'round the world, like lone folk, –
    None to talk with – always single!

EDITH M. THOMAS

CHRISTMAS EVE REMEMBERED

I see them going to the chapel
To confess their sins, Christmas Eve
In a parish in Monaghan.
Poor parish! And yet memory does weave
For me about these folk
A romantic cloak.

No snow, but in their minds
The fields and roads are white.
They may be talking of the turkey markets
Or foreign politics, but tonight
Their plain, hard country words
Are Christ's singing birds.

38

Bicycles scoot by, old women
Cling to the grass margin,
Their thoughts are earthy but their minds move
In dreams of the Blessed Virgin
For one in Bethlehem
Has kept their dreams safe for them.

"Did you hear from Tom this Christmas?"
"These are the dark days."
"Maguire's shop did a great trade,
Turnover double – so Maguire says."
"I can't delay now Jem
Lest I be late for Bethlehem."

Like this my memory saw
Like this my childhood heard
These pilgrims of the North.
And memory, you have me spared
A light to follow them
Who go to Bethlehem.

PATRICK KAVANAGH

THE OXEN

Christmas Eve, and twelve of the clock.
  "Now they are all on their knees,"
An elder said as we sat in a flock
  By the embers in hearthside ease.

We pictured the meek mild creatures where
  They dwelt in their strawy pen,
Nor did it occur to one of us there
  To doubt they were kneeling then.

So fair a fancy few would weave
  In these years! Yet, I feel,
If someone said on Christmas Eve,
  "Come; see the oxen kneel

"In the lonely barton by yonder coomb
  Our childhood used to know,"
I should go with him in the gloom,
  Hoping it might be so.

THOMAS HARDY

40

THIS HOLY NIGHT

God bless your house this holy night,
  And all within it;

God bless the candle that you light
  To midnight's minute:

The board at which you break your bread,
  The cup you drink of:

And as you raise it, the unsaid
  Name that you think of:

The warming fire, the bed of rest,
  The ringing laughter:

These things, and all things else be blest
  From floor to rafter

This holy night, from dark to light,
  Even more than other;

And, if you have no house tonight,
  God bless you, brother.

ELEANOR FARJEON

CHRISTMAS EVE AT SEA

A wind is rustling "south and soft,"
  Cooing a quiet country tune,
The calm sea sighs, and far aloft
  The sails are ghostly in the moon.

Unquiet ripples lisp and purr,
  A block there pipes and chirps i' the sheave,
The wheel-ropes jar, the reef-points stir
  Faintly – and it is Christmas Eve.

The hushed sea seems to hold her breath,
  And o'er the giddy, swaying spars,
Silent and excellent as Death,
  The dim blue skies are bright with stars.

Dear God – they shone in Palestine
  Like this, and yon pale moon serene
Looked down among the lowing kine
  On Mary and the Nazarene.

JOHN MASEFIELD

MINSTREL'S SONG
FROM *The Coming of the Kings*

I've just had an astounding dream as I lay in the straw.
I dreamed a star fell on to the straw beside me
And lay blazing. Then when I looked up
I saw a bull come flying through a sky of fire
And on its shoulders a huge silver woman
Holding the moon. And afterwards there came
A donkey flying through that same burning heaven
And on its shoulders a colossal man
Holding the sun. Suddenly I awoke
And saw a bull and a donkey kneeling in the straw,
And the great moving shadows of a man and a woman –
I say they were a man and a woman but
I dare not say what I think they were. I did not dare to look.
I ran out here into the freezing world
Because I dared not look. Inside that shed.

A star is coming this way along the road.
If I were not standing upright, this would be a dream.
A star the shape of a sword of fire, point-downward,
Is floating along the road. And now it rises.
It is shaking fire on to the roofs and the gardens.
And now it rises above the animal shed
Where I slept till the dream woke me. And now
The star is standing over the animal shed.

TED HUGHES

AWAKE! GLAD HEART!

Awake! glad heart! get up and sing!
It is the birthday of thy King.
  Awake! awake!
  The sun doth shake
Light from his locks, and, all the way
Breathing perfumes, doth spice the day.

Awake! awake! hark how th'wood rings,
Winds whisper, and the busy springs
  A concert make!
  Awake! awake!
Man is their high-priest, and should rise
To offer up the sacrifice.

I would I were some bird, or star,
Fluttering in woods, or lifted far
  Above this inn,
  And roar of sin!
Then either star or bird should be
Shining or singing still to thee.

HENRY VAUGHAN

A CHRISTMAS CAROL

Before the paling of the stars,
   Before the winter morn,
   Before the earliest cock-crow
Jesus Christ was born:
    Born in a stable,
   Cradled in a manger,
In the world His hands had made
    Born a stranger.

Priest and King lay fast asleep
   In Jerusalem,
Young and old lay fast asleep
   In crowded Bethlehem:
Saint and Angel, ox and ass,
   Kept a watch together,
   Before the Christmas daybreak
   In the winter weather.

Jesus on his Mother's breast
   In the stable cold,
Spotless Lamb of God was He,
   Shepherd of the fold:
Let us kneel with Mary Maid,
   With Joseph bent and hoary,
With Saint and Angel, ox and ass,
   To hail the King of Glory.

CHRISTINA ROSSETTI

THE ANIMALS' CAROL

Christus natus est! the cock   Christ is born
Carols on the morning dark.

Quando? croaks the raven stiff   When?
Freezing on the broken cliff.

Hoc nocte, replies the crow   This night
Beating high above the snow.

Ubi? ubi? booms the ox   Where?
From its cavern in the rocks.

Bethlehem, then bleats the sheep   Bethlehem
Huddled on the winter steep.

Quomodo? the brown hare clicks,   How?
Chattering among the sticks.

Humiliter, the careful wren   Humbly
Thrills upon the cold hedge-stone.

Cur? cur? sounds the coot   Why?
By the iron river-root.

Propter homines, the thrush   For the sake of man
Sings on the sharp holly-bush.

Cui? cui? rings the chough   To whom?
On the strong, sea-haunted bluff.

Mary! Mary! calls the lamb   Mary
From the quiet of the womb.

Praeterea ex quo? cries   Who else?
The woodpecker to pallid skies.

Joseph, breathes the heavy shire   Joseph
Warming in its own blood-fire.

Ultime ex quo? the owl   Who above all?
Solemnly begins to call.

De Deo, the little stare   Of God
Whistles on the hardening air.

Pridem? pridem? the jack snipe   Long ago?
From the stiff grass starts to pipe.

Sic et non, answers the fox   Yes and no
Tiptoeing the bitter lough.

Quomodo hoc scire potest?
Boldly flutes the robin redbreast.

How do I know this?

Illo in eandem, squeaks
The mouse within the barley-sack.

By going there

Quae sarcinae? asks the daw
Swaggering from head to claw.

What luggage?

Nulla res, replies the ass,
Bearing on its back the Cross.

None

Quantum pecuniae? shrills
The wandering gull about the hills.

How much money?

Ne nummum quidem, the rook
Caws across the rigid brook.

Not a penny

Nulla resne? barks the dog
By the crumbling fire-log.

Nothing at all?

Nil nisi cor amans, the dove
Murmurs from its house of love.

Only a loving heart

Gloria in Excelsis! Then
Man is God, and God is Man.

CHARLES CAUSLEY

50

SLEEP, BABY, SLEEP!

Sleep, baby, sleep! the Mother sings:
Heaven's angels kneel and fold their wings.
Sleep, baby, sleep!

With swathes of scented hay thy bed
By Mary's hand at eve was spread.
Sleep, baby, sleep!

At midnight came the shepherds, they
Whom seraphs wakened by the way.
Sleep, baby, sleep!

And three kings from the East afar
Ere dawn came guided by a star.
Sleep, baby, sleep!

They brought thee gifts of gold and gems
Rich orient pearls, pure diadems.
Sleep, baby, sleep!

But thou who liest slumbering there
Art King of kings, earth, ocean, air.
Sleep, baby, sleep!

Sleep, baby, sleep! the shepherds sing:
Through heaven, through earth, hosannas ring
Sleep, baby, sleep!

JOHN ADDINGTON SYMONDS

MICE IN THE HAY

out of the lamplight
  whispering worshipping
the mice in the hay

 timid eyes pearl-bright
  whispering worshipping
whisking quick and away

they were there that night
  whispering worshipping
smaller than snowflakes are

quietly made their way
  whispering worshipping
close to the manger

yes, they were afraid
  whispering worshipping
as the journey was made

from a dark corner
  whispering worshipping
scuttling together

But He smiled to see them
  whispering worshipping
there in the lamplight

stretched out His hand to them
  they saw the baby King
hurried back out of sight
  whispering worshipping

LESLIE NORRIS

52

A CHRISTMAS CAROL

The Christ-child lay on Mary's lap,
    His hair was like a light.
(O weary, weary were the world,
    But here is all aright.)

The Christ-child lay on Mary's breast,
    His hair was like a star.
(O stern and cunning are the kings,
    But here the true hearts are.)

The Christ-child lay on Mary's heart,
    His hair was like a fire.
(O weary, weary is the world,
    But here the world's desire.)

The Christ-child stood at Mary's knee,
    His hair was like a crown,
And all the flowers looked up at him,
    And all the stars looked down.

G. K. CHESTERTON

MARY'S LULLABY
FROM *The Gift of a Lamb*

Sleep, King Jesus,
Your royal bed
Is made of hay
In a cattle-shed.
Sleep, King Jesus,
Do not fear,
Joseph is watching
And waiting near.

Warm in the wintry air
You lie,
The ox and the donkey
Standing by,
With summer eyes
They seem to say:
Welcome, Jesus,
On Christmas Day!

Sleep, King Jesus:
Your diamond crown
High in the sky
Where the stars look down.
Let your reign
Of love begin,
That all the world
May enter in.

CHARLES CAUSLEY

I SAW THREE SHIPS

I saw three ships come sailing in
    On Christmas day, on Christmas day;
I saw three ships come sailing in
    On Christmas day in the morning.

And what was in those ships all three
    On Christmas day, on Christmas day;
And what was in those ships all three
    On Christmas day in the morning?

Our Saviour Christ and his lady,
    On Christmas day, on Christmas day;
Our Saviour Christ and his lady,
    On Christmas day in the morning.

Pray whither sailed those ships all three
    On Christmas day, on Christmas day;
Pray whither sailed those ships all three
    On Christmas day in the morning?

O they sailed into Bethlehem
    On Christmas day, on Christmas day;
O they sailed into Bethlehem
    On Christmas day in the morning.

And all the bells on earth shall ring
    On Christmas day, on Christmas day;
And all the bells on earth shall ring
    On Christmas day in the morning.

And all the angels in heaven shall sing
    On Christmas day, on Christmas day;
And all the angels in heaven shall sing
    On Christmas day in the morning.

And all the souls on earth shall sing
  On Christmas day, on Christmas day;
And all the souls on earth shall sing
  On Christmas day in the morning.

Then let us all rejoice amain
  On Christmas day, on Christmas day;
Then let us all rejoice amain
  On Christmas day in the morning.

TRADITIONAL

57

SNOW IS FALLING

Snow is falling, snow is falling.
Reaching for the storm's white stars,
Petals of geraniums stretch
Beyond the window bars.

Snow is falling, all is chaos,
Everything is in the air,
The angle of the crossroads,
The steps of the back stair.

Snow is falling, not like flakes
But as if the firmament
In a coat with many patches
Were making its descent.

As if, from the upper landing,
Looking like a lunatic,
Creeping, playing hide-and-seek,
The sky stole from the attic.

Because life does not wait,
Turn, and you find Christmas here.
And a moment after that
It's suddenly New Year.

Snow is falling, thickly, thickly.
Keeping step, stride for stride,
No less quickly, nonchalantly,
Is that time, perhaps,
Passing in the street outside?

And perhaps year follows year
Like the snowflakes falling
Or the words that follow here?

Snow is falling, snow is falling,
Snow is falling, all is chaos:
The whitened ones who pass,
The angle of the crossroads,
The dazed plants by the glass.

BORIS PASTERNAK
translated by Jon Stallworthy &
Peter France

SNOW-BOUND

Shut in from all the world without,
We sat the clean-winged hearth about,
Content to let the north-wind roar
In baffled rage at pane and door,
While the red logs before us beat
The frost-line back with tropic heat;
And ever, when a louder blast
Shook beam and rafter as it passed,
The merrier up its roaring draught
The great throat of the chimney laughed.

JOHN GREENLEAF WHITTIER

CHRISTMAS DAY

Nature's decorations glisten
   Far above their usual trim;
Birds on box and laurels listen
   As so near the cherubs hymn.

Boreas now no longer winters
   On the desolated coast;
Oaks no more are riv'n in splinters
   By the whirlwind and his host.

Spinks and ouzles sing sublimely,
   "We too have a Saviour born,"
Whiter blossoms burst untimely
   On the blest Mosaic thorn.

God all-bounteous, all-creative,
   Whom no ills from good dissuade,
Is incarnate, and a native
   Of the very world he made.

CHRISTOPHER SMART

BALLADE

So much the goat scratches he can't sleep,
So much the pot takes water it breaks,
So much you heat iron it turns red,
So much you hammer it it cracks,
So much a man's worth as he's esteemed,
So much is he away he's forgotten,
So much is he bad he's despised,
So much you cry Noël that it comes.

So much you talk you contradict yourself,
So much fame's worth as it gets you favors,
So much you promise you take it back,
So much you beg you're given what you sought,
So much a thing's expensive everyone wants it,
So much you go after it you get it,
So much it's common it loses its charm,
So much you cry Noël that it comes.

So much you love a dog you feed it,
So much a song's heard it catches on,
So much fruit's hoarded up it goes rotten,
So much you dispute a place it's already taken,
So much you dawdle you ruin your life,
So much you hurry you run out of luck,
So much you hold on you lose your grip,
So much you cry Noël that it comes.

So much you joke you quit laughing,
So much you spend you lose your shirt,
So much you're honest you go broke,
So much is "here" worth as a thing promised,
So much you love God you go to church,
So much you give you're obliged to borrow,
So much the wind shifts it blows cold at last,
So much you cry Noël that it comes.

Prince, so much a fool lives he wises up,
So much he travels he comes back home,
So much they beat him he knows he was wrong,
So much you cry Noël that it comes.

FRANÇOIS VILLON
translated by Galway Kinnell

THE PRAYER OF DAFT HARRY

Lord, since this world is filled with fire,
    Inside this rounded mould –
Let's turn it inside out, O Lord,
    While hands and feet are cold.

Let's split the world in half, O Lord,
    As open as my palm,
Until the snow has melted down,
    And hands and feet are warm.

Let's turn the world all inside out,
    And glorify Our Name;
Until Our fire makes Jesus laugh,
    While I blow up the flame.

Let's do it now, this minute, Lord,
    And make a glorious blaze:
Till Jesus laughs and claps his hands,
    While Mary sings Our praise!

W. H. DAVIES

SHEPHERDS' CAROL

Three practical farmers from back of the dale —
    Under the high sky —
On a Saturday night said "So long" to their sheep
That were bottom of dyke and fast asleep —
    When the stars came out in the Christmas sky.

They called at the pub for a gill of ale —
    Under the high sky —
And they found in the stable, stacked with the corn,
The latest arrival, newly-born —
    When the stars came out in the Christmas sky.

They forgot their drink, they rubbed their eyes —
    Under the high sky —
They were tough as leather and ripe as a cheese
But they dropped like a ten-year-old down on their knees —
    When the stars came out in the Christmas sky.

They ran out in the yard to swap their news —
    Under the high sky —
They pulled off their caps and roused a cheer
To greet a spring lamb before New Year —
    When the stars came out in the Christmas sky.

NORMAN NICHOLSON

TO A SNOWFLAKE

What heart could have thought you? —
Past our devisal
(O filigree petal!)
Fashioned so purely,
Fragilely, surely,
From what Paradisal
Imagineless metal,
Too costly for cost?
Who hammered you, wrought you,
From argentine vapour? —
"God was my shaper.
Passing surmisal,
He hammered, He wrought me,
From curled silver vapour,
To lust of His mind:—
Thou could'st not have thought me!
So purely, so palely,
Tinily, surely,
Mightily, frailly,
Insculped and embossed,
With His hammer of wind,
And His graver of frost."

FRANCIS THOMPSON

THE BIRDS

When Jesus Christ was four years old,
The angels brought Him toys of gold,
Which no man ever had bought or sold.

And yet with these He would not play.
He made Him small fowl out of clay,
And Blessed them till they flew away:
    Tu creasti Domine.

Jesus Christ, Thou child so wise,
Bless mine hands and fill mine eyes,
And bring my soul to Paradise.

HILAIRE BELLOC

CAROL OF THE BROWN KING

Of the three Wise Men
Who came to the King,
One was a brown man,
So they sing.

Of the three Wise Men
Who followed the Star,
One was a brown king
From afar.

They brought fine gifts
Of spices and gold
In jewelled boxes
Of beauty untold.

Unto His humble
Manger they came
And bowed their heads
In Jesus' name.

Three Wise Men,
One dark like me –
Part of His
Nativity.

LANGSTON HUGHES

KINGS CAME RIDING

Kings came riding
   One, two and three,
Over the desert
   And over the sea.

One in a ship
   With a silver mast;
The fishermen wondered
   As he went past.

One on a horse
   With a saddle of gold;
The children came running
   To behold.

One came walking,
   Over the sand,
With a casket of treasure
   Held in his hand.

All the people
   Said, "where go they?"
But the kings went forward
   All through the day.

Night came on
   As those kings went by;
They shone like the gleaming
   Stars in the sky.

CHARLES WILLIAMS

HIGH IN THE HEAVEN

FROM *The Gift of a Lamb*

High in the heaven
A gold star burns
Lighting our way
As the great world turns.

Silver the frost
It shines on the stem
As we now journey
To Bethlehem.

White is the ice
At our feet as we tread,
Pointing a path
To the manger-bed.

CHARLES CAUSLEY

WINTER SONG

The browns, the olives, and the yellows died,
And were swept up to heaven; where they glowed
Each dawn and set of sun till Christmastide,
And when the land lay pale for them, pale-snowed,
Fell back, and down the snow-drifts flamed and flowed.

From off your face, into the winds of winter,
The sun-brown and the summer-gold are blowing;
But they shall gleam again with spiritual glinter,
When paler beauty on your brows falls snowing,
And through those snows my looks shall be soft-going.

WILFRED OWEN

WINTER NIGHT

Pile high the hickory and the light
Log of chestnut struck by the blight.
Welcome in the winter night.

The day has gone in hewing and felling,
Sawing and drawing wood to the dwelling
For the night of talk and story-telling.

These are the hours that give the edge
To the blunted axe and the bent wedge,
Straighten the saw and lighten the sledge.

Here are question and reply,
And the fire reflected in the thinking eye.
So peace, and let the bob-cat cry.

EDNA ST. VINCENT MILLAY

EDDI'S SERVICE

Eddi, priest of St. Wilfrid
    In the chapel at Manhood End,
Ordered a midnight service
    For such as cared to attend.

But the Saxons were keeping Christmas,
    And the night was stormy as well.
Nobody came to service,
    Though Eddi rang the bell.

"Wicked weather for walking,"
    Said Eddi of Manhood End.
"But I must go on with the service
    For such as care to attend."

The altar-lamps were lighted, —
    An old marsh-donkey came,
Bold as a guest invited,
    And stared at the guttering flame.

The storm beat on at the windows,
    The water splashed on the floor,
And a wet, yoke-weary bullock
    Pushed in through the open door.

"How do I know what is greatest,
    How do I know what is least?
That is my Father's business,"
    Said Eddi, Wilfrid's priest.

"But — three are gathered together —
    Listen to me and attend.
I bring good news, my brethren!"
    Said Eddi, of Manhood End.

And he told the Ox of a manger,
  And a stall in Bethlehem,
And he spoke to the Ass of a Rider
  That rode to Jerusalem.

They steamed and dripped in the chancel.
  They listened and never stirred,
While, just as though they were Bishops,
  Eddi preached them The Word.

Till the gale blew off on the marshes
  And the windows showed the day.
And the Ox and the Ass together
  Wheeled and clattered away.

And when the Saxons mocked him.
  Said Eddi of Manhood End,
"I dare not shut His chapel
  On such as care to attend."

RUDYARD KIPLING

CAROL FOR THE LAST CHRISTMAS EVE

The first night, the first night,
   The night that Christ was born,
His mother looked in his eyes and saw
   Her maker in her son.

The twelfth night, the twelfth night,
   After Christ was born,
The Wise Men found the child and knew
   Their search had just begun.

Eleven thousand, two fifty nights,
   After Christ was born,
A dead man hung in the child's light
   And the sun went down at noon.

Six hundred thousand or thereabout nights,
   After Christ was born,
I look at you and you look at me
But the sky is too dark for us to see
   And the world waits for the sun.

But the last night, the last night,
   Since ever Christ was born,
What his mother knew will be known again,
And what was found by the Three Wise Men,
And the sun will rise and so may we,
   On the last morn, on Christmas Morn,
Umpteen hundred and eternity.

NORMAN NICHOLSON

MANGERS

Who knows the name and country now,
  Of that rich man who lived of old;
Whose horses fed at silver mangers,
  And drank of wine from troughs of gold?

He who was in a manger born,
  By gold and silver undefiled —
Is known as Christ to every man,
  And Jesus to a little child.

W. H. DAVIES

THE HOLLY AND THE IVY

The holly and the ivy,
  When they are both full grown,
Of all the trees that are in the wood,
  The holly bears the crown.

The rising of the sun
  And the running of the deer,
The playing of the merry organ,
  Sweet singing in the choir.

78

The holly bears a blossom
  As white as lily flower,
And Mary bore sweet Jesus Christ
  To be our sweet saviour.

The rising of the sun, etc.

The holly bears a berry
  As red as any blood,
And Mary bore sweet Jesus Christ
  To do poor sinners good.

The rising of the sun, etc.

The holly bears a prickle
  As sharp as any thorn,
And Mary bore sweet Jesus Christ
  On Christmas day in the morn.

The rising of the sun, etc.

The holly bears a bark
  As bitter as any gall,
And Mary bore sweet Jesus Christ
  For to redeem us all.

The rising of the sun, etc.

The holly and the ivy,
  When they are both full grown,
Of all the trees that are in the wood
  The holly bears the crown.

The rising of the sun, etc.

TRADITIONAL

79

CHRISTMAS

What, do they suppose that everything has been said that *can* be said about any one Christmas thing?

About beef, for instance?
About mince-pie?
About ivy?
About mistletoe?
About hunt-the-slipper?
About blind-man's buff?
About thread-the-needle ?
About puss-in-the-corner?
About forfeits?
About the bell-man?
About chilblains?
About the fire?
About school-boys?
About Christmas boxes?
About Hogmanay?
About mumming?
About brown?
About hoppy-horse?
About wakes?
About hackin?
About going-a-gooding?
About Julklaps? (*who has exhausted the subject, we should like to know?*)
About elder-wine?
About cards?
About gifts?
About Twelfth-cake?
About characters?
About aldermen?

About all being in the wrong?
About all being in the right?
About plum-pudding?
About holly?
About rosemary?
About Christmas Eve?
About hot cockles?
About shoeing-the-wild-mare?
About he-can-do-little-that-can't-do-this?
About snap-dragon?
About Miss Smith?
About the waits?
About carols?
About the clock on it?
About their mothers?
About turkeys?
About goose-pie?
About saluting the apple-trees?
About plum-porridge?
About hoppings?
About "feed-the-dove"?
About Yule-dough?
About loaf-stealing?
About wad-shooting?
About pantomime?
About New-Year's Day?
About wassail?
About king and queen?

About eating too much?　　　　　About charity?
About the doctor?　　　　　　　About faith, hope and endeavour?

About the greatest plum-pudding for the greatest number?

LEIGH HUNT

81

CHRISTMASTIDE

Love came down at Christmas,
    Love all lovely, Love Divine;
Love was born at Christmas,
    Star and Angels gave the sign.

Worship we the Godhead,
    Love Incarnate, Love Divine;
Worship we our Jesus:
    But wherewith for sacred sign?

Love shall be our token,
    Love be yours and love be mine,
Love to God and all men,
    Love for plea and gift and sign.

CHRISTINA ROSSETTI

A CHRISTMAS CRADLE

Let my heart the cradle be
Of Thy bleak Nativity!
Tossed by wintry tempests wild,
If it rock Thee, Holy Child,
Then, as grows the outer din,
Greater peace shall reign within.

JOHN BANISTER TABB

CHRISTMAS TREES BURN IN THE FOREST WITH GILDED FLAMES

Christmas trees burn in the forest with gilded flames,
toy wolves glare from the bushes —

O my prophetic sadness,
O my calm freedom,
and the dead crystal vault of heaven laughing without end!

OSIP MANDELSTAM
translated by Clarence Brown & W. S. Merwin

NEW YEAR

The New Year's unwritten page we view
As a lea field to plough and sow
The memory of weeds from the last
Turned page comes through
But only matters what this year we grow.

PATRICK KAVANAGH

THE BLESSING OF THE NEW YEAR

God, bless to me the new day,
Never vouchsafed to me before;
It is to bless Thine own presence
Thou hast given me this time, O God.

Bless Thou to me mine eye,
May mine eye bless all it sees;
I will bless my neighbour,
May my neighbour bless me.

God, give me a clean heart,
Let me not from sight of Thine eye;
Bless to me my children and my wife,
And bless to me my means and my cattle.

TRADITIONAL, SCOTTISH GAELIC
translated by Alexander Carmichael

THE ANGEL THAT PRESIDED

The Angel that presided o'er my birth
Said, "Little creature, formed of joy and mirth,
Go love without the help of any thing on earth."

WILLIAM BLAKE

THE BORING ORBIT

My daughter who's not yet born and whose name is *Hagar*
asked me: "Daddy, why does the earth go round?"
"Early one morning God woke up
And the angel Gabriel brought Him His morning coffee.
'One sugar, please.'
God stirred the sugar with his gold spoon
In dull, empty circles,
Dull circles,
Dull, empty circles.
And since that time, my child,
The earth's been rotating in its boring orbit."

SAMIH AL-QASIM
translated by Abdullah al-Udhari

NOTHINGMAS DAY

No it wasn't.

It was Nothingmas Eve and all the children in Notown were not
tingling with excitement as they lay unawake in their heaps.
D
  o
    w
      n
        s
          t
            a
              i
                r

        s their parents were busily not placing the last
crackermugs, glimmerslips and sweetlumps on the Nothingmas
Tree.

Hey? But that was that invisible trail of chummy sparks or
vaulting stars across the sky
> Father Nothingmas – drawn by 18 or 21
> rainmaidens!
> Father Nothingmas – his sackbut bulging with air!
> Father Nothingmas – was not on his way!

(From the streets of the snowless town came the quiet of
unsung carols and the merry silence of the steeple bell.)

Next morning the children did not fountain out of bed with
cries of WHOOPERATION! They picked up their Nothingmas
Stockings and with traditional quiperamas such as: "Look what
I haven't got! It's just what I didn't want!" pulled their stockings
on their ordinary legs.

For breakfast they ate – breakfast.

After woods they all avoided the Nothingmas Tree, where Daddy, his face failing to beam like a leaky torch, was not distributing gemgames, sodaguns, golly-trolleys, jars of humdrums and packets of slubberated croakers.

Off, off, off went the children to school, soaking each other with no howls of "Merry Nothingmas and a Happy No Year!", and not pulping each other with no-balls.

At school Miss Whatnot taught them how to write No Thank You Letters.

Home they burrowed for Nothingmas Dinner.
The table was not groaning under all manner of
      NO TURKEY
      NO SPICED HAM
      NO SPROUTS
      NO CRANBERRY JELLYSAUCE
      NO NOT NOWT
There was not one (1) shoot of glee as the Nothingmas Pudding, unlit, was not brought in. Mince pies were not available, nor was there any demand for them.

Then, as another Nothingmas clobbered to a close, they all haggled off to bed where they slept happily never after.

    and that is not the end of the story. . . . . . .

ADRIAN MITCHELL

87

INDEX OF POETS

INDEX OF TITLES AND FIRST LINES

Titles are in *italics*. Where the title and the first line are the same, the first line only is listed.

89

ACKNOWLEDGMENTS

We would like to thank all the authors, publishers and literary representatives, who have given permission to reprint poems in this collection. Every effort has been made to contact copyright holders, and we apologize for any inadvertent omissions.

Samih al-Qasim: to Penguin Books Ltd for "The Boring Orbit" from MODERN POETRY OF THE ARAB WORLD translated and edited by Abdullah al-Udhari (Penguin Books, 1986) selection and introduction copyright © Abdullah al-Udhari, 1986, first published in Arabic in Haifa, 1983; this translation first published in VICTIMS OF A MAP (ed. Abdullah al-Udhari) by ALSAQI Books, 1984: copyright © Samih al-Qasim, 1983; translation copyright © Abdullah al-Udhari, 1984.

Hilaire Belloc: to The Peters Fraser & Dunlop Group Ltd for "The Birds" from THE COMPLETE VERSE OF HILAIRE BELLOC (Pimlico, a division of Random Century).

George Mackay Brown: to John Murray (Publishers) Ltd for "A Child's Calendar" from SELECTED POEMS.

Charles Causley: to David Higham Associates Limited for "High in the Heaven" and "Mary's Lullaby" from THE GIFT OF A LAMB (Robson Books, 1978) and "The Animals' Carol" from COLLECTED POEMS 1951-1975, (Macmillan 1975).

Elizabeth Coatsworth: to Catherine B. Barnes for "On a Night of Snow" from NIGHT AND THE CAT (Macmillan N.Y., 1950).

e.e. cummings: to MacGibbon & Kee, an imprint of HarperCollins Publishers Limited for "little tree" from THE COMPLETE POEMS 1913-1962. "little tree" is reprinted from TULIPS & CHIMNEYS by e.e. cummings, edited by George James Firmage, by permission of Liveright Publishing Corporation. Copyright 1923, 1925 and renewed 1951, 1953 by e.e. cummings. Copyright © 1973, 1976 by the Trustees for the e.e. cummings Trust. Copyright © 1913, 1976 by George James Firmage.

Eleanor Farjeon: to David Higham Associates Limited for "This Holy Night" from SOMETHING I REMEMBER, ed. Anne Harvey (Blackie).

Robert Frost: to the Estate of Robert Frost and Jonathan Cape as publisher and Henry Holt and Company, Inc., for "Stopping By Woods On A Snowy Evening" from THE POETRY OF ROBERT FROST, edited by Edward Connery Lathem. Copyright 1942, 1951 by Robert Frost. Copyright © 1970 by Lesley Frost Ballantine. Copyright 1923, © 1969 by Henry Holt and Company, Inc.

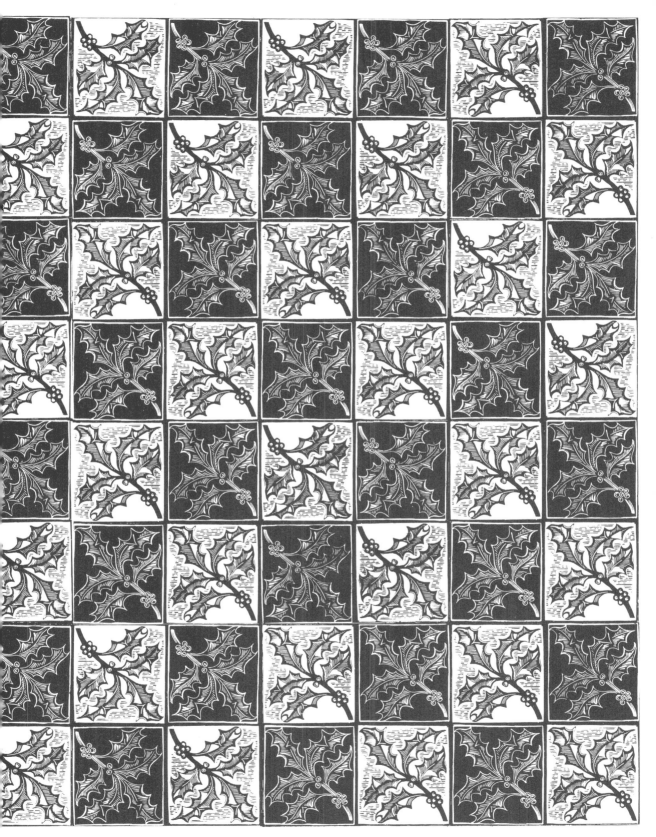

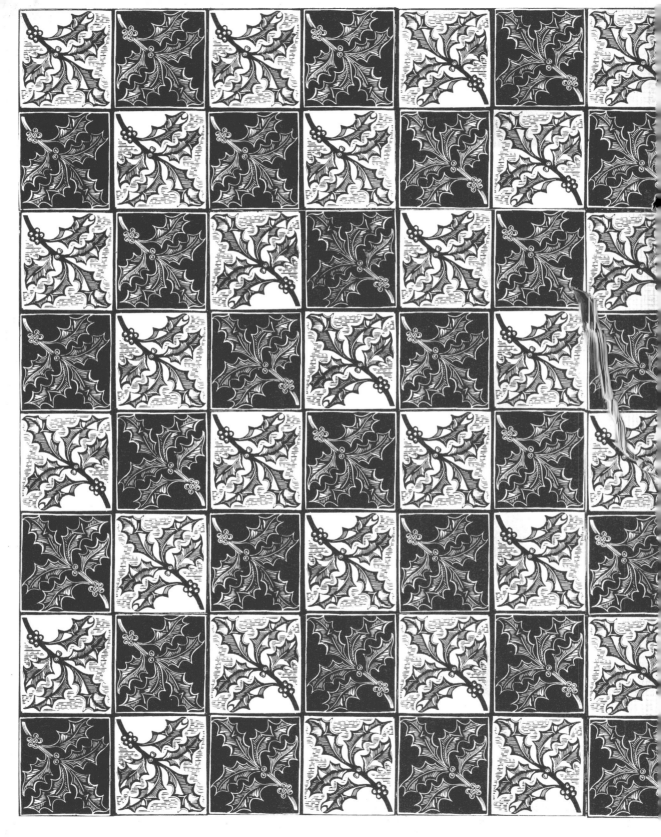